OLD CRUMP

The True Story of a Trip West

by **LAURIE LAWLOR**

illustrations by **JOHN WINCH**

HOLIDAY HOUSE / New York

For Megan and John,
best of travelers always
—L. L.

For Jessie, who shared the
2001 Journey out West
— J. W.

Library of Congress Cataloging-in-Publication Data
Lawlor, Laurie.
Old Crump: the true story of a trip West;
pictures by John Winch.—1st ed.
p. cm.
Summary: In 1850, a faithful ox helps a group of travelers survive
their trip through Death Valley.
ISBN 0-8234-1608-9 (hardcover)
1. Oxen—Juvenile fiction. [1. Oxen—fiction. 2. Survival—Fiction.
3. Death Valley (Calif. and Nev.)—Fiction. 4.West (U.S.)—Fiction.]
I. Winch, John, 1944– ill. II. Title.
PZ10.3.L 3894 01 2002
[E]—dc21   2001016943

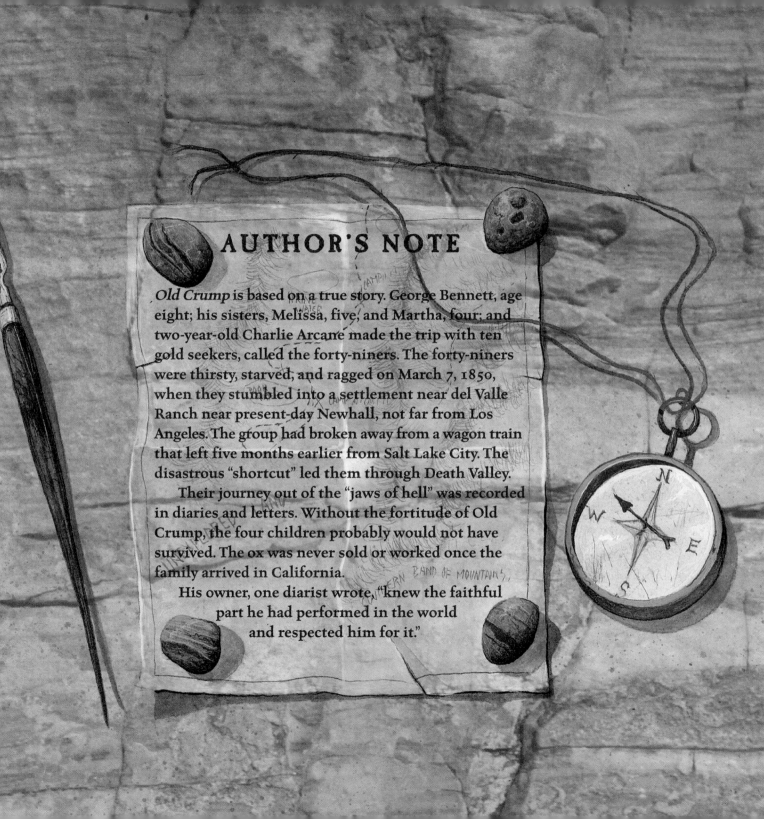

AUTHOR'S NOTE

Old Crump is based on a true story. George Bennett, age eight; his sisters, Melissa, five, and Martha, four; and two-year-old Charlie Arcane made the trip with ten gold seekers, called the forty-niners. The forty-niners were thirsty, starved, and ragged on March 7, 1850, when they stumbled into a settlement near del Valle Ranch near present-day Newhall, not far from Los Angeles. The group had broken away from a wagon train that left five months earlier from Salt Lake City. The disastrous "shortcut" led them through Death Valley.

Their journey out of the "jaws of hell" was recorded in diaries and letters. Without the fortitude of Old Crump, the four children probably would not have survived. The ox was never sold or worked once the family arrived in California.

His owner, one diarist wrote, "knew the faithful part he had performed in the world and respected him for it."

FAITHFUL OLD CRUMP pulled our wagon across the plains
to the peaks we named Mount Misery and Too High.
"Where's California?" Charlie asked.
"Far away," Ma replied.

Old Crump plodded on,
following the place where the sun went down each night.
When we stopped to camp,
we sang songs and danced.

Days passed. Our flour and salt pork dwindled.
No one had much use for fiddle music.

"Where's California?" Charlie asked.
Ma sighed. "Keep moving," she said.
When we reached the top of a divide,
Pa stopped and looked down.

"There it is," he said. "Death Valley."
And, oh, what a desolate place!
Wind-beaten, treeless hills
and everywhere: awful silence.

That night cold wind blew from the north.
We burned our wagons to make a fire to keep warm.
Every treasured belonging from home: gone.

The sun made us squint.
Rocks bit through
what was left of our shoes.
Ma crumbled bits of sugar for us to hold
in our mouths so we wouldn't think
so much about our thirst
or empty stomachs.

"Can't go any farther," Charlie cried.
Little Martha didn't say anything.
When the journey had begun,
she'd scampered lively as a quail.
Now she was slower'n a jill poke.

Ma took two strong hickory shirts still left
and turned them inside out.
She sewed each shirt together to make two pockets
for Martha and Charlie to ride Old Crump,
one on either side.

Melissa and I climbed up on Old Crump's broad back and held on with a strap. "Get along, Old Crump!" Pa cried. And the faithful ox moved forward slow and steady. Never a stumble or a fall.

After a few miles, the other oxen bucked and kicked.
Their riders screamed and pitched headlong into the sand.
Melissa and I jumped off Old Crump.
Ma grabbed the little ones
just in case Old Crump got frisky, too.
He didn't. He flicked his tail,
stomped his hoof, and looked at us
with his big gentle eyes.

On and on we rode, even though there was nothing
but a few bunches of rattling dried grass
for Old Crump to eat.
Overhead, rainless clouds looked
like grazing herds of white oxen.

"Water!" somebody cried.
We rushed toward that shining lake as fast as we could.
But when we arrived, all we found was a shallow pool of brine.
Nothing but a mirage.

Canteens empty. No water. No grass. No fuel.
Some spoke of killing oxen for food.
"Don't touch Old Crump!" Pa warned.
"We're hungry!" the men replied.
"Who will carry the children?" Pa asked. "You?"
The men did not answer. They turned away, ashamed.
Even so, Melissa and I kept watch all night
to make sure Old Crump stayed safe.

"Get along, Old Crump!" Pa said the next day.
And the faithful ox moved forward, slow and steady, never a stumble or a fall.
At last we reached the end of the sandy wasteland.
"Good-bye, Death Valley!" Ma whispered.
We climbed mountains again and the air filled with spicy juniper and pine.

We spied a roof in the valley below. Another mirage?
No. "California!" Charlie cried.
When we reached the house, a woman came outside.
She looked at us ragged and thin atop Old Crump.
"*Mucha pobre*," she said, and shook her head.
From her pockets, she gave us each an orange.
I held the cool, sweet orange to my cheek
and rolled it against my closed eyes.
For once, the sun's glare seemed
to disappear.

That night we ate a feast
of tortillas, beans, milk, and cheese.
The next day, we traveled
to our new home beside the ocean.

Pa kept his word.
He never sold Old Crump or let anyone harm him.
Now fat and sleek, the faithful ox grazes
with our cattle in San Joaquin Valley.
Old Crump stomps his hoof.
When we pat him, he looks at us with big gentle eyes.
And I know he remembers our long journey
and how he carried us, slow and steady, never a stumble or a fall.